ROMAN BRITAIN

Usborne Quicklinks

The Usborne Quicklinks website is packed with thousands of links to all the best websites on the internet. The websites include information, video clips, sounds, games and animations that support and enhance the information in Usborne internet-linked books.

To visit the recommended websites for this book, go to the Usborne Quicklinks website at **www.usborne.com/quicklinks** and enter the keywords **Roman Britain**.

When using the internet please follow the internet safety guidelines displayed on the Usborne Quicklinks website. The recommended websites in Usborne Quicklinks are regularly reviewed and updated, but Usborne Publishing Ltd. is not responsible for the content or availability of any website other than its own. We recommend that children are supervised while using the internet.

ROMAN BRITAIN

Ruth Brocklehurst & Abigail Wheatley

Illustrated by Ian McNee & Giacinto Gaudenzi

Designed by Anna Gould & Stephen Moncrieff

Edited by Jane Chisholm

Consultant: Dr. Andrew Gardner,
University College, London

Contents

Britain and the Roman empire

Around 2,000 years ago, life in Britain was dramatically shaken up when a powerful force invaded from across the sea – the Romans came, saw and, eventually, conquered.

From their magnificent city of Rome, the Romans had built up a mighty army and conquered more and more land until they ruled over the biggest empire of ancient times. For 400 years, most of Britain was part of that empire – daily life, culture, language and even the British landscape would never be the same again.

Romans invade

By 58BC the Romans dominated the Mediterranean region, from the deserts of North Africa and Syria to the Pyrenees. In the lands beyond Italy, which they called the provinces, the Romans imposed not only their laws and their hefty taxes, but also their way of life and their language, Latin.

The expanding empire

The great Roman army general Julius Caesar and his troops were fighting to secure the Roman province of *Gaul* (France). Britain, which the Romans called *Britannia*, lay tantalizingly close, on what many Romans believed to be the edge of the world. To capture these lands would surely be to conquer the world. But Caesar had practical motives too.

Britain was reported to be rich in gold and silver and its tribesmen disorganized and quarrelsome. Added to this, some southern Britons were supporting rebels in Gaul who were resisting Roman rule. Caesar calculated that conquering both Britain and Gaul would be a tremendous boost to his career – at a minimal risk.

HIBERNIA
(Ireland)

CALEDONIA
(Scotland)

BRITANNIA

This map, based on one from the 2nd century, shows what the Romans thought the British Isles looked like. You can also see the names the Romans used for the different parts of the British Isles.

Caesar attacks!

When Caesar first invaded Britain in 55BC, storms drove part of his army back to Gaul. He won some battles in the southeast of the country, but was surprised by the Britons' skilled use of chariots in combat. It was not the easy fight he had expected. Gales wrecked many of his ships on the beaches where they had landed and he was forced to retreat.

Caesar returned the next year, in 54BC, but he soon had to go back to Gaul to deal with a revolt. This wasn't the last the Britons would hear of the Romans, though. Nearly a hundred years later, Roman forces invaded again and eventually conquered all but the highlands of Scotland.

In the year 40, an insane Roman Emperor, Caligula, wanted to invade Britain. But he stopped at the French coast, where he ordered his men to collect shells to prove his 'conquest' of the sea!

British warriors watch from the cliffs of Kent as Caesar's army approaches.

According to some stories, Caesar brought 800 warships with him in 54BC.

Tribal Britons

The Romans weren't very impressed by the tribesmen of 1st century Britain. They saw the Britons as barbarians – often drunk and always fighting. While the Romans had been busy conquering a vast empire, building magnificent cities and developing a sophisticated culture, the people of Britain were leading a simpler rural life.

This bronze helmet is a fine example of British Iron Age metalwork – but it was probably made for show, rather than for fighting.

British living

Most Britons lived in small settlements in distinctive round houses made from wood plastered with mud, dung and straw. Even their fortifications – huge hilltop fortresses, called hillforts – were simply made from earth and wood or piled-up rocks.

This helped to confirm the Romans' view that Britain was a primitive and uncivilized place. What they didn't appreciate was that the Britons had a thriving culture, were highly skilled in many crafts including metalworking, and had trading contacts all over northern Europe.

When archaeologists at Butser Ancient Farm, in Hampshire, reconstructed these round houses, they found them surprisingly warm and weatherproof.

Round houses didn't have windows, so they were built with the doors facing east, to let in the morning sun.

A divided land

Because people in Britain and northern Europe, including Gaul, spoke a group of similar, Celtic languages, they could understand each other easily, and had much in common. But they had little sense of belonging to one nation, as they lived in separate tribes that often competed – and even fought – against one another.

After Caesar's attempted invasions, southern British tribes had much closer contact with the Romans in Gaul. Some tribes even paid taxes to Rome, in return for protection.

But one tribe, the Catuvellauni, led by an ambitious chief called Caratacus, began to capture more and more territory from surrounding tribes. Around the year 40, Verica, the king of the Atrebates tribe, fled to Rome to ask for help. This gave the Romans the excuse they needed to invade Britain again.

Cornovii
Caereni   Lugi
Smertae
Carnonacae
Decantae
                        Taezali
Creones
Vacomagi
Caledones
            Venicones
Epidii
Damnonii   Votadini
Selgovae
Novantae
            Brigantes

                        Parisi

Gangani
            Deceangli   Coritani
Ordovices Cornovii
                        Iceni
                        Catuvellauni
Demetae   Dobunii
Silures   Trinovantes
            Atrebates Cantiaci
Dumnonii Durotriges Belgae

This map shows the different tribal areas in 1st century Britain.

Claudius conquers

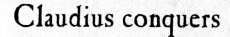

The Emperor Claudius brought several war elephants to Britain as part of his army. The local people must have been terrified.

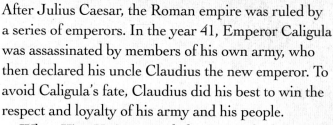

After Julius Caesar, the Roman empire was ruled by a series of emperors. In the year 41, Emperor Caligula was assassinated by members of his own army, who then declared his uncle Claudius the new emperor. To avoid Caligula's fate, Claudius did his best to win the respect and loyalty of his army and his people.

When King Verica appealed to Rome for help, Claudius seized his chance. He was determined to prove himself a strong ruler by conquering Britain once and for all.

This scene shows a British hillfort under siege. The wooden fortress is protected by rings of deep ditches and massive earth mounds up to 24m (80ft) high.

Roman archers shoot flaming arrows into the hillfort, to burn it down.

Britons hurl rocks at their attackers.

This smaller catapult, like a crossbow, is called a *scorpio*.

Roman soldiers use their shields to form a protective shell, known as the *testudo*, or tortoise.

Huge catapults, like this one, called a *ballista*, shoot boulders and heavy iron-tipped bolts over great distances.

10

River raids

Claudius ordered a massive number of troops – around 40,000 in all – to invade Britain. They landed on the southeast coast and marched inland until they reached a river. Caratacus and his army were waiting for them on the other side.

While both armies prepared for battle, the shrewd Roman general, Plautius, sent a team of crack troops downstream, with special instructions. They swam quietly across the river on horseback, to launch a surprise raid on the Britons. Meanwhile, the rest of the army crossed the river upstream, also unnoticed, and attacked the Britons from behind. It was a decisive Roman victory.

Britons under siege

Next, another general, Vespasian, advanced along the south coast, and laid siege to as many as 20 British hillforts. During these sieges, the Romans would surround the forts and subject them to merciless missile attacks, pounding the wood and earth walls with huge stones and bolts from massive catapults – until the Britons were forced to surrender.

Roman victory

Once most of the south was in Roman hands, Vespasian sent for the Emperor. Barely four months after the invasion began, Claudius and his legions marched in to capture the Catuvellauni stronghold at Colchester. Just two weeks later, Claudius returned to Rome, to a hero's welcome. There was a triumphal procession through the city to celebrate his conquest of *Britannia*.

"I had horses, men and weapons: is it any wonder I was unwilling to lose them? Just because you Romans want to rule everyone, does that mean everyone should accept slavery?"

Speech by Caratacus, imagined by the Roman historian, Tacitus, in his book, *The Annals*.

Freedom fighter

Caratacus was eventually caught and paraded through the streets of Rome in chains. But Claudius was so impressed with his dignity, he gave him his freedom.

Battling Boudicca

Over the next 30 years, the Romans gradually conquered most of southern England, but they often met fierce opposition. To help keep order, the Romans gave local tribal leaders jobs in government and allowed them to keep their land, in return for their loyalty.

But the Romans soon learned that they couldn't control the British against their will. In the year 60, they faced an uprising so serious that it nearly spelled the end of Roman rule.

Trouble brewing

One of the British leaders who was loyal to the Romans was Prasutagus, King of the Iceni tribe in East Anglia. On his deathbed, he divided his kingdom between his daughters and the Roman emperor. But the Roman authorities ignored his wishes, seizing the Iceni lands and all their possessions. When Prasutagus' wife Boudicca protested, she was whipped in the middle of the village and her daughters were raped. The Queen was furious – this was war!

Boudicca immediately raised a vast rebel army of men, women and children – all keen to drive out the occupying forces. They headed for Colchester, the Roman capital, and ransacked the city, killing thousands of people and destroying anything that represented Rome.

Then they turned on the Roman cities of *Londinium* (London) and *Verulamium* (St. Albans), and burned them to the ground in a ferocious assault.

This British warrior's shield was found in the Thames at Battersea in London. It dates from just before the time of Boudicca's rebellion.

Legends say that, after Boudicca's defeat, she and her daughters poisoned themselves to avoid being captured by the Romans.

The last battle

Meanwhile, most of the Roman army in Britain was hundreds of miles away in northern Wales, fighting another rebellious group, the Druids. When news of Boudicca's revolt came through, the army rushed back to deal with it.

Boudicca's 200,000 troops far outnumbered the Romans' 10,000, but the Britons stood little chance against the professional Roman fighters. The Romans advanced in tight formation, wading through the Britons, who turned and fled. It was a chaotic bloodbath in which Roman chroniclers claimed 80,000 Britons died.

Trapped

Boudicca's fleeing fighters were hemmed in by their own wagons, where their families had parked to watch the battle.

Hill

10,000 Romans

Forest

Forest

200,000 Britons

British wagons

The Britons sound elaborately shaped bronze war trumpets as they charge into battle.

The most important warriors ride on swift war chariots. Some women fight beside the men.

Military might

The key to the Romans' success in conquering so much of Britain so quickly was the virtually unstoppable power of their army. Not only was it the largest military force of its time, but its men were the most strictly organized, best equipped and most highly trained fighters of their day.

At its largest, the Roman army had over 300,000 men. To keep such a vast fighting machine running like clockwork, it had to be strictly regimented. So it was divided into units called legions. Each legion had over 5,000 foot soldiers, or legionaries, organized into groups of 80, known as centuries. With a clear chain of command, every man knew his place and exactly what was expected of him.

Roman legionaries were led into battle by officers with large banners.

A soldier's life

Legionaries were the elite soldiers of Roman times. To be eligible, a man had to be over 17, literate, tall and very fit. At first, only Roman citizens – men born in Rome or Italy – could become legionaries; non-citizens were known as auxiliaries.

In return for 20-26 years' service, a legionary earned a good wage and learned a trade, such as engineering or medicine. If he proved brave and loyal, he could rise up the ranks to become a *centurion*, the officer in command of a century.

Boot camp

When they joined up, all legionaries were issued with a kit that gave them the cutting edge over their enemies. Each man had a short sword called a *gladius*, a dagger and a spear-like javelin. For protection in battle, legionaries were given a metal breastplate, a helmet and a large curved shield. They also carried cooking utensils and tools for building temporary battle camps.

Roman soldiers had to keep super fit. As well as perfecting their javelin throwing, swordcraft and tactical moves, they also went on three training marches a month, marching over 30km (18 miles) in just five hours. No wonder the average legionary went through three pairs of boots a year!

Roman soldiers carried swords and large shields, like the ones shown here.

A general commanded several legions.

A legate was in charge of a legion.

A centurion led a century (80 men).

A legionary was a citizen foot soldier.

A cavalry officer fought on horseback.

A non-citizen fighter was called an auxiliary.

Keeping the peace

Once Roman rule was established in Britain, the role of the army changed from an invading force, to a peacekeeping one. Now its main job was to defend the country against attacks from hostile tribes and to enforce Roman law. Soldiers kept in training, and they also had non-military duties, working as engineers, accountants, cooks and vets. But, before they did anything else, they had to build themselves a fort.

Standard plan

The largest forts were almost like small towns, with everything the soldiers needed – from barrack blocks and bathhouses, to hospitals and stables. They all followed the same rectangular plan, which meant men could always find their way around – whether they were in Manchester, Mainz or Mesopotamia. The three legions based in Britain lived in fortresses in Caerleon, York and Chester. But there were many other forts for smaller units dotted around the country.

This bronze helmet was found at the site of Ribchester Roman Fort, in Lancashire. A soldier would have worn it for training exercises.

This aerial photograph shows the remains of Housesteads Roman Fort in Northumberland. You can still see the outline of some of its buildings inside the fortified outer walls.

Food store

Officers' headquarters

Lookout tower

Hospital

Originally, five barrack blocks and a workshop stood in this part of the fort.

Commanding officer's house

Settling down

Many soldiers made friends with the locals, teaching them the Roman way of life, but adopting British customs too. When they retired, they often settled near their old forts, and even married local women.

Over time, British and Roman cultures became more and more mixed. Britons could also become 'Romanized' by joining the army themselves. For some, this was a chance to travel and experience life in other parts of the empire.

Letters from home

A treasure trove of hundreds of written records has been found in the ruins of the Vindolanda Roman Fort at Chesterholm. These provide an amazingly detailed picture of the daily lives of soldiers in Roman Britain.

Among the documents that have survived are duty rosters that describe soldiers working as shoemakers, brewers, builders and medics. There are also letters sent to and from soldiers. They include party invitations, deals with local traders – and even a letter from a mother sending her soldier son socks and underpants from home.

Barrack blocks

Main street

Main gateway

There were more barrack blocks here.

Latrines (communal lavatories)

Roman soldiers sent to Britain had to adapt to the chilly climate. This razor handle, shaped like a legionary's leg, shows the thick socks that soldiers wore under their sandals.

Road works

According to the proverb, all roads lead to Rome. This was literally true in the Roman empire, as the Romans built roads out from their capital city to each new territory they conquered. They were used to good, straight roads, but the only ones in Britain were dirt tracks. So, the army started right away on a massive campaign of building, to provide a brand new network of over 16,000km (10,000 miles) of roads.

This scene shows a Roman engineer using a device called a *groma*, to make sure he plots a straight course for a new road. He looks along the *groma* arms to make sure the next marker is in a straight line with the previous one.

Straight forward

Roads were vital for governing the province, as they helped troops to march quickly to wherever they were needed. They also made it much easier and faster to send messages between the forts, and to transport supplies. Eventually, there were roads connecting all the Romans forts and towns. Even today, several of the most important main roads in Britain still follow the routes of the original Roman ones.

Roman roads usually followed the most direct route possible, which often meant they went in a straight line. In fact they're famous for being incredibly straight – although they did bend around immovable obstacles such as marshes or steep hills.

Gravel sandwich

This diagram shows the layers of materials the Romans often used when building roads in Britain.

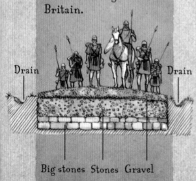

Drain

Drain

Big stones   Stones   Gravel

The soldiers who built the roads used special surveying equipment to help them lay out a straight route. Then, construction work began. The work team dug a deep ditch, to make room for strong foundations. Then they filled it with layers of differently sized stones, all packed down tightly. The finished road had a humped surface with ditches on either side, so that rainwater would run off and drain away.

Finished roads were measured carefully, to give an accurate idea of how long it would take to travel along them. The Romans calculated distances in Roman miles, which were 1,000 paces long – equivalent to just under a modern mile, or around 1.5km.

The engineer's assistant adjusts the position of the marker as instructed by the engineer.

Building bridges

To complement their extensive network of roads, the Romans also needed bridges to carry them safely across Britain's many rivers. During campaigns, when time was short, they made temporary bridges by fastening together a line of boats and placing a wooden walkway on top. More permanent bridges were constructed from wood or stone. Roman soldiers tested their stability by marching across them in formation.

This is a Roman milestone from Wales. Stones like this one, showing the distance to nearby towns or forts, were placed every mile along Roman roads.

Town life

To the Romans, the only civilized way to live was in towns. But the Britons didn't have any, so the Romans got building. Like Roman forts, every town followed a similar design. Streets were laid out in a grid, dividing the town into blocks known as *insulae*. At the heart of every town was the *forum*, a busy market square where people met to do business and catch up on the news. The *forum* was lined with shops on three sides. On the fourth side stood the Roman equivalent of the town hall, the *basilica*.

This scene shows the bustling market square, or *forum*, of a regional Roman town.

The town council held its meetings in this building, the *basilica*.

British temple

Town houses

A wealthy Roman would have lived in a large, luxurious town house, or *domus*. But most people lived in small houses in the *insulae*, working in trades and services. They sold their wares – from metalwork and pottery to meat and bread – from shops at the front of their houses, and lived at the back or upstairs.

Law and order

The Romans divided Britain into regions called *civitates*. Each had a main town with a council of local leaders in charge of taxes, law, public buildings and roads. By involving Britons in local government, the Romans hoped to avoid rebellions. During the 3rd century (years 200-300) many towns had walls built around them. These weren't just for protection; they showed off a town's importance and helped soldiers to control the traffic going in and out.

Roman temple

In an *insula*

This cutaway view shows how traders' houses in the Roman *insulae* were divided up. Families lived in the upper rooms...

...and used the lower rooms as workshops and trading outlets.

Retirement homes

Some towns, known as *coloniae*, were built to house Roman army veterans, and served as regional capitals. Colchester, York, Lincoln and Gloucester were all *coloniae*. Soldiers were given land there as part of their pensions.

Bathtime

Clean routine

Britons had always washed with soap, but instead the Romans rubbed perfumed oil into their skin.

Then they exercised to work up a sweat and scraped off the oil, sweat and grime using a curved tool called a *strigil*.

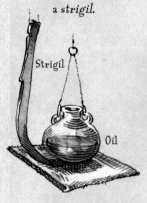

Strigil

Oil

The focus of social life in every Romano-British town was its public bathhouse. There, for a small fee, people could scrub and scrape, pamper and preen, and wash away the cares of the day. They could also work out in the exercise yard, unwind with a massage or catch up on the gossip over a relaxing game of dice.

The bathhouse consisted of a series of rooms of different temperatures. The bathing ritual usually began with a dip in a tepid pool in a room known as the *tepidarium*. The bather then moved to the steamy *calderium* to soak in a hot tub. Finally, the routine was finished with a refreshing swim in the cold, outdoor pool or *frigidarium*.

The Roman baths at Bath can still be seen today, although much of the building was reconstructed in the 19th century.

Many wealthy people paid slaves to do their scrubbing and scraping for them.

Aquae Sulis

One of the most magnificent bathhouses in Roman Britain was in the spa town of *Aquae Sulis*, now called Bath, where cleanliness and godliness came together – literally. Long before Roman times, Britons had visited its hot spring to worship Sulis, the water goddess of healing and wisdom.

The Romans linked Sulis with their own goddess, Minerva, who also had healing powers. So they built a temple by the sacred spring and dedicated it to Sulis-Minerva.

Later, a large bathhouse was added to the temple, using the naturally heated water from the spring. People visited from all over Europe, making Bath one of the liveliest and holiest towns in Roman Britain. Even today, the spring in the Roman baths is so hot you can see the steam rising from the water.

These Roman dice were found in the remains of a Roman bathhouse in London. Other games similar to backgammon were popular bathtime amusements.

As well as aqueducts and pipes, the Romans used other inventions to move water around in Britain.

They built chains of buckets, turned by big wooden wheels, to lift water up from the bottom of wells...

...and they created sturdy stone-built sewers under their streets, to take all their waste water away.

But the Romans weren't always so clever. They sometimes made water pipes from lead, which probably gave them mild lead poisoning.

Civil engineering

Roman forts, roads, bridges and towns were impressive enough. But Roman builders and engineers also equipped their great stone buildings and settlements with an array of gadgets that were all designed to make life safer, cleaner and much more comfortable. To the Britons, Roman technology must have seemed the ultimate in civilization.

Clean and clear

Running water was a basic necessity for the Romans. They invested a great deal of time, energy and ingenuity in finding reliable ways to transport it from mountain springs and streams down to their forts, towns and even their most important houses.

Back in Rome, water was brought to cities in stone-built channels, known as aqueducts, which were often raised on monumental stone arches. But in Britain, aqueducts were more modest channels that snaked along the ground and were often made from wood. Within towns, water was distributed in wooden pipes joined together with metal. The water supplied public drinking fountains, baths in public bathhouses and public toilets.

Built in stone

In some parts of Britain, people already used local stone to make buildings, but the Romans did things on a much grander scale. By gluing stones together with cement, they could make their walls much higher and thicker. They also built arches, which the Britons had never seen before.

24

Fire down below

Many Roman-style buildings in Britain had under-floor central heating, provided by a *hypocaust* system. This was a furnace that circulated hot air through specially constructed spaces under the floors and within the walls. *Hypocaust* heating was used for grand private houses and for bathhouses in towns and forts. Well-off people could also pay for tiled floors and even window glass to make their homes snug and bright.

Sea safety

The Romans also built tall lighthouses near their most important ports. These were sturdy towers with a place at the top for lighting a fire to guide ships safely in and out of ports at night.

During the daytime, the towers doubled as lookout stations, where soldiers could keep watch for pirates and raiders. To the Britons, it must have seemed that the Romans had tamed the elements.

This is a Roman lighthouse, which still stands on the coast at Dover in Kent. The orangey lines are clay tiles, laid in layers to strengthen the stone walls.

London town

The area occupied by Roman Londinium is now the financial district of modern London, known as The City.

This is an artist's impression of London in 120. Most of the city grew up on the north bank of the Thames, but a small trading settlement also developed on the south bank.

Londinium

London didn't exist before the Romans came to Britain; it was no more than a few farms scattered along the River Thames. But when Claudius invaded in 43, his men built a bridge across the Thames and put up a fort to guard it. Soon, local traders and craftsmen settled near the fort and a town grew up on the north bank of the river.

In Roman times, the Thames was wider than it is today, and deep enough for ships to sail right up to the bridge, where a port was built. This made the river a useful trading link between Britain and the rest of the empire. Within ten years, London – which the Romans called *Londinium* – had established itself as a thriving, cosmopolitan merchant town.

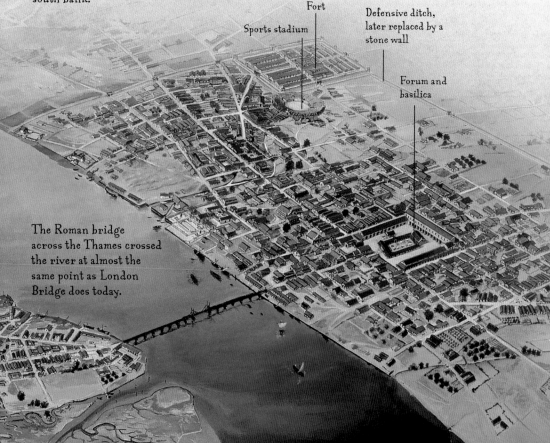

Sports stadium

Fort

Defensive ditch, later replaced by a stone wall

Forum and basilica

The Roman bridge across the Thames crossed the river at almost the same point as London Bridge does today.

Britain's first capital

Another town that grew rapidly during the early days of Roman rule in Britain was Colchester. In 49, the Romans had made it into a *colonia*, a town for Roman settlers and ex-soldiers. It soon became the first capital of the Roman province of Britain.

Then, in the year 60, Colchester and London were burned to the ground by Boudicca and her rebels. Both towns were quickly rebuilt, but Colchester's old tribal connections made it politically unstable. London, sited on the Thames, was more convenient for trade and transportation. So, gradually the Romans moved their headquarters to London.

Imperial London

By the turn of the 1st century, building work had begun to transform London into an imperial city, boasting a grand basilica and a forum even larger than Trafalgar Square. Later, an imposing city wall was added, to defend the capital. At the heart of the country's commercial and political life, London flourished and became one of the great cities of the Roman empire.

Power base

A few Roman emperors did visit Britain, but most of the time the province was run by a governing council, based in London. It was led by a governor, who was head of the army and chief justice. But to make sure he didn't become too powerful, the emperor appointed another official, called a *procurator*, to collect taxes and control the country's finances.

Luxury imports

Londinium was a destination for merchant ships importing goods that weren't made in Britain. Here are some of the things they brought:

Wine, olive oil and fish sauce from Italy and Spain

Glossy red pottery from France

Fine glass from Germany and Italy

Perfumes and spices from Egypt and the Middle East

The Roman peace

Some experts think this mountain in northeast Scotland, Bennachie, is the site of Agricola's great Scottish victory. The Romans called Scotland *Caledonia*.

Welsh blade

This Roman sword was found in the Roman fort of Segontium at Caernarfon in north Wales. The fort was first occupied in 77.

Once the Romans had settled in southern Britain and introduced the Roman way of life, they felt fairly secure. In return for benefits such as running water, regular markets and a reliable justice system, the local people were expected to cooperate with their new governors and obey Roman laws. They were still allowed to run their own tribes and follow their own religions – but on Roman terms.

The Romans had used this same system to bring peace and stability to the rest of their empire. It was so effective that this period became known as the *pax Romana*, or Roman peace. The Romans moved swiftly and ruthlessly against anything that threatened this peace. They had learned their lesson from the horrors of Boudicca's rebellion.

North and west

In the year 71, when the Brigantes tribe began to create unrest in northern England, the Romans reacted fast. The Roman army marched north, defeating the Brigantes and building forts in the area to strengthen their position. This gave them a secure base for pushing further north and west.

28

Agricola's army

But the most decisive move came in 77, with the arrival of a new Roman governor named Julius Agricola. He led a series of bold campaigns, finishing off the last lingering resistance from the Brigantes and advancing across Wales and Scotland.

Agricola moved his troops forward at an amazing pace, coordinating the movements of soldiers on foot, on horseback and even on ships, so that they all met up at the right time and place for their next attack. He also took advantage of British fighting skills, allowing Britons to join his troops if they had proved themselves loyal to Rome.

The tide turns

By 83, Agricola's troops had won a great victory in the northeast highlands of Scotland and had secured their control over a large area. They even began to look at Ireland with eager eyes, convinced that Rome could go on expanding forever. But not all of these gains were to last.

In 84, Agricola was called back to Rome by the emperor, Domitian. Some Romans believed that Domitian was jealous of Agricola's achievements. But perhaps he simply realized that Agricola was spreading his troops too thinly across too wide an area in Britain, creating serious problems for the control of the province.

Whatever the real reason, many Roman troops also left Britain at this time to defend other parts of the empire. The Romans withdrew from Scotland, and never gained as much ground there again. But at least they had strengthened their grip on Wales and England.

Agricola's campaign

We know a lot about Agricola because his son-in-law, a Roman writer named Tacitus, wrote about his career.

According to Tacitus, Agricola won over British chiefs by teaching them about Roman customs.

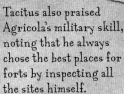

Tacitus also praised Agricola's military skill, noting that he always chose the best places for forts by inspecting all the sites himself.

Agricola died suddenly in Rome. Tacitus believed that he had been poisoned by the emperor Domitian out of jealousy.

29

Hadrian's wall was built from the materials that were available nearby.

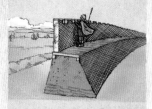

Where stone was scarce, the builders mounded up earth and covered it in turf – earth and grass.

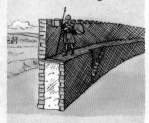

Elsewhere, the wall was built in longer-lasting stone blocks. Stone was also used to replace the turf section later on.

Much of Hadrian's Wall survives today, and can still be seen snaking its way across the north of England.

Hadrian's Wall

Many Romans saw their withdrawal from Scotland as a temporary setback. There was no reason, they thought, why they couldn't keep extending their territory in Britain until they had conquered the whole island.

But in the year 117 there was a new Roman emperor, Hadrian, and he had other plans. He spent more than two thirds of his rule in the provinces and believed it was more important for the Romans to strengthen and defend the land they already had, than to conquer new territories. In 122, he visited Britain, where he set his ideas in stone.

Stonewalling

Hadrian realized that the fierce northern tribes weren't about to give up their land easily. Their constant attacks on the Romans were also draining valuable time and resources from the army. So Hadrian ordered a fortified frontier wall to be built, to protect Roman Britain. This allowed the army to control who crossed the border. It was also a potent symbol of the power of Rome.

Hadrian's legacy

Hadrian's Wall was the largest structure in the Roman empire and an impressive feat of engineering. It was 120km (75 miles) long, stretching right across the country, between the rivers Tyne and Solway. Along the wall there were sixteen forts, with smaller forts, called milecastles, every Roman mile in between. There were lookout turrets too, so soldiers could keep watch and pass messages between forts if they spotted trouble.

Within months of Hadrian's death in 138, his successor, Antoninus Pius, attacked Scotland again. By 142, he had captured southern Scotland, so he began building a new frontier wall across the country. The 'Antonine Wall' was about half the length of Hadrian's and was mostly built from blocks of turf, instead of stone. But, less than 20 years later, local tribes rebelled, forcing the Romans back behind Hadrian's Wall. This remained the northern frontier for the next 250 years.

This head is all that's left of a 2m (6.5ft) tall statue of Hadrian that stood in London in around 122.

This section of Hadrian's Wall leads to Housesteads, one of the best preserved forts.

Tin trade

Throughout the ancient world, Cornwall was famous for producing tin. But the Romans had tin mines in Spain that were easier for them to get to, so they never really bothered with the Cornish mines.

This scene shows the village of Chysauster in Cornwall. The Britons who lived here piled up stones to make the walls of their round houses, and were probably from the Dumnonii tribe.

Life on the edge

Hadrian's Wall marked the official limit of the Roman empire in Britain. Beyond it, the tribes of Scotland were free from Roman interference, in theory at least. But even inside the wall, parts of Wales and the far west and north of England were so remote, that they gained little from the advantages of Roman civilization, even though the Romans were technically in charge.

Distant corners

While Britons in the south of England had adopted many of the Roman ways, tribes in the wilder parts of the west and the north continued to live much as they had before the Romans arrived. The main difference was they were no longer allowed to carry weapons.

Most still lived in round houses on small settlements and raised animals and grew crops for a living. Beyond the few Roman roads, travel was still slow and difficult, and people stayed close to home, only dimly aware of events in the wider empire.

Border country

When it came to the native Britons, both inside and beyond the boundaries of the empire, the Romans were generally prepared to live and let live. But local tribes just to the north of Hadrian's Wall could expect swift Roman raids if they stepped out of line – even if they didn't, the Romans kept a careful watch on them. If they wanted to trade with the Romans, they had to cross the wall, give up their weapons and pay taxes to the Romans on all their goods.

Free Caledonia

Further north into Scotland – the land the Romans knew as *Caledonia* – the tribes were harder to control. There, the Romans resorted to bribery, trade and diplomacy. They paid the more powerful tribal leaders with money, luxury gifts and privileges so that they wouldn't stir up trouble.

This gradually caused great changes in the region. The Romans never succeeded in conquering these tribes, but over time they began to merge together under just a few powerful leaders recognized by the Romans. This made them stronger, but their old way of life had come to an end – for good.

Painted people

One of the most powerful groups to emerge in Scotland were a people known by the Romans as *Picts*, or *painted ones*, because of the tattoos they were supposed to have had on their skin. The Picts were farmers who lived in central and northern Scotland, and were known for their ferocious raids on Roman-held areas of Britain.

"Let us, at the first encounter, prove what heroes Caledonia has in reserve – untouched, unconquered, ready to fight for freedom without regret."

Speech by Calgacus, a Scottish tribal leader, imagined by the Roman historian Tacitus, in his book, *Agricola*.

This standing stone was carved by Pictish craftsmen, and shows Pictish warriors, some of them on horseback.

33

The same money was used all over the Roman empire, which made trade fairer and easier. Here are some of the most common coins.

A gold *aureus* – the most valuable Roman coin

A silver *denarius* – there were 25 in an *aureus*

A bronze *sestertius* – there were 4 in a *denarius*

A bronze *dupondius* – there were 2 in a *sestertius*

A copper *as* – there were 2 in a *dupondius*

A bronze *semis* – there were 2 in an *as*

A copper *quadrans* – there were 4 in an *as*

Market forces

The new Romanized lifestyle in most of Britain led to an industrial boom, as craftsmen and merchants rushed to meet the demand for new products from around the Roman empire. The road system boosted local trade, making it easier than ever before to move goods around the country. International trade flourished too, as British products could now be transported as far away as Syria or Africa, in exchange for exotic foreign produce. The Roman empire soon became one great marketplace.

All at sea

The Romans had a vast fleet of merchant ships to transport goods all around the empire. Roman sailors didn't have any instruments to help them to navigate the seas. So they judged their position by the sun, moon and stars, and consulted books which recorded the best routes and times to travel. Storms were a terrible danger for the Romans' small wooden merchant ships, so they tried to sail only during the calmer spring and summer months. Pirates were also a constant worry. Even so, it was often quicker and easier to transport goods by sea than overland.

Checks and balances

Fair trade depended on everyone using the standard, Roman system of weights and measures throughout the empire. So roman merchants weighed their goods carefully, using special scales they carried with them. Legionaries also inspected the weights used in the markets to make sure that customers weren't being cheated by unscrupulous traders.

Made in Britain

One of the main reasons the Romans invaded Britain was for the metals mined there. In Roman Britain these were used to make everything from coins to army helmets and pipes for plumbing. Industries, such as pottery and the wool trade, also grew under the Romans. Most British goods were sold locally, but some were exported. One of the most prized British exports was a hooded cloak called a *birrus Britannicus*.

Map key

This map shows where different goods came from around the empire. Roman lands are shaded green.

- Grain
- Olive oil
- Wine
- Salt
- Cloth
- Pottery
- Metals
- Glass
- Wood
- Marble
- Purple dye
- Hunting dogs
- Cattle
- Horses
- Wild animals

CALEDONIA

HIBERNIA

North Sea

BRITANNIA

Atlantic Ocean

GERMANIA

GAUL

HISPANIA

Rome

ITALIA

Black Sea

ASIA

AFRICA

CYPRUS

SYRIA

Mediterranean Sea

EGYPT

ARABIA

Far from home

"The climate is objectionable, with its frequent rain and mists, but there is no extreme cold."

The Roman historian Tacitus, who wrote about Britain and its history in the 1st century.

It wasn't only goods and money that passed between Britain and the remotest corners of the empire. People also came and went – whether it was soldiers sent to Britain to keep the peace, traders bringing exotic goods, or British slaves shipped out as a profitable export.

Many of the legionary soldiers, administrators and traders who came to Britain were from Rome itself. For them it must have seemed a wet, chilly and distant land – and some complained about the clouds of mosquitoes that swarmed through the marshy land of the Thames in summer, and the illnesses they carried with them.

World travels

The Roman army also brought in extra troops, known as auxiliaries, from other parts of the empire, including Gaul, Spain, Germany, North Africa and the Near East. Later, fewer Romans wanted to sign up for the army. So troops from as far as Romania and Assyria arrived to join the British legions, while British recruits were sent to Spain, Armenia and Egypt, as well as to Rome itself.

Apart from soldiers, all sorts of other people chose to settle in Britain – from traders to people with special skills, such as doctors and teachers from Greece and sculptors from Gaul. But probably the largest numbers of people moving through Britain were slaves.

This is a carving of a legionary soldier, found in London. He may have come from Rome. You can see the warm cloak wrapped close around his neck.

36

These are Roman slave chains, found in Kent.

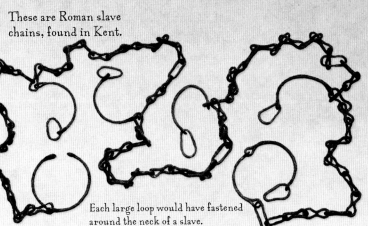

Each large loop would have fastened around the neck of a slave.

Slave stories

A tombstone from South Shields shows that Regina, a British slave woman, was happily married to a merchant who had come all the way from Palmyra in Syria.

A strip of wood found at Hadrian's Wall preserves a letter sent by a slave named Severus. He wrote to another slave, Candidus, about buying food supplies for a feast.

A wooden tablet found in London records the sale of Fortunata, a slave woman from northern France. She was bought by another slave who had a high-up job in the government of Britain.

The slave trade

In many parts of the world in Roman times, it was common to use slaves for the dirtiest, most difficult and dangerous jobs. But the Romans turned slavery into an international business. When Julius Caesar conquered Gaul, he brought back a million people with him as slaves. They would have been sold at slave markets in Rome and throughout the empire.

The Romans made slaves of anyone they captured in war, but they also made some criminals into slaves as a punishment. When times were desperately hard, some Britons probably sold their relatives or even themselves as slaves.

Sometimes being a slave wasn't so bad. Those with useful skills might get comfortable jobs with kind families or in government. But others were so badly treated they ran away, or died from working in terrible conditions. We know very little about British slaves, as most Romans didn't think slaves were worth mentioning in their written records.

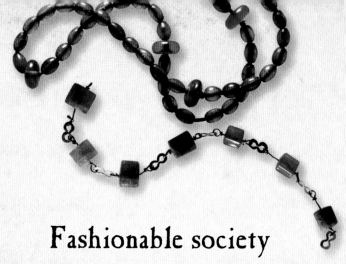

All that glitters
Men and women all piled
on the jewels. Accessories
like these gold rings
showed off your wealth
and status.

But brooches and pins
weren't just fashion
statements – they kept
your clothes on. This
dragon brooch in a Celtic
design would have
fastened a cloak.

Fashionable society

Romano-British society had a strict pecking order,
which showed in the way people dressed. Slaves, who
didn't count as citizens and had no rights, wore very
simple clothing, and ordinary citizens dressed little
better than their slaves. But people with wealth and
power liked to flaunt it, adorning themselves with the
finest fabrics and the most glittering gems.

Whatever their age, sex or social status, all
Romano-Britons wore a basic garment called a tunic.
It was made from two rectangles, or T-shapes, of
woollen or linen cloth, sewn at the sides and shoulders,
often tied around the waist with a belt or cord.

Celtic chic

Before the Romans came along, the Britons had their
own style of dress. While the Romans wore plain
clothes in sober shades, the Britons liked bold stripes
and plaids, in as many gaudy shades of russet, yellow,
blue and purple as possible. They decorated their
clothes with embroidered designs and fastened them
with large, decorative brooches and belt buckles.

Under Roman influence, Britons began to dress more
like their new rulers, but they still kept some of their
native styles too, adding distinctive Celtic touches to
Roman outfits.

Power dressing

For formal events, men wore a *toga*, a large semicircle of cloth, draped carefully over the tunic. *Togas* were complicated to put on, and so heavy that men had to walk very slowly in them. This looked dignified, but it wasn't very practical – so *togas* were usually only worn by rich men with a leisurely lifestyle. A *toga* was a status symbol. Most men wore undyed *togas*, but politicians were allowed to wear a *toga* with a purple band. Only the emperor could dress all in purple.

The purple stripe on this man's *toga* shows he is a politician.

The woman having her hair done wears a dress called a *stola* over her tunic.

The head of this bone hairpin shows a very elaborate hairstyle that was considered the very height of fashion in the 1st century.

Hairdressing

The Roman emperor and his wife, the empress, set the trends right across the empire. Under Roman rule, men were usually clean-shaven and cut their hair short. But when Emperor Hadrian was depicted on a coin wearing a full beard, many men copied his style.

Women's hairstyles usually involved sweeping long hair into a bun. Slave girls spent hours styling their mistresses' hair in more and more elaborate buns, sometimes using hair pieces, decorated with hairpins and piles of false curls.

Sports and spectacles

To keep their subjects happy and loyal, Roman emperors and officials put on spectacular public shows in every town. These entertainments were often staged as part of public holidays or religious festivals and included plays and chariot races. But most popular of all were the sensational, often very violent, sporting shows, known simply as the games.

The games were held in a large stadium on the edge of town, often with enough seats for the entire local population. A day at the games began with a grand procession of all the performers around the oval arena. This was followed by animal fights, mock hunts, wrestling matches, public executions and finally gladiator combats.

This is how Caerleon Amphitheatre, in South Wales, may have looked during the 2nd century. It has enough seating for an audience of 6,000.

Outside the main arena, people buy snacks and trinkets or watch other entertainments.

Special guests, including local politicians, sit in an enclosed area, where they can enjoy the best views of the games.

Gladiators

The highlights of the games were undoubtedly the gladiator combats. Gladiators were slaves or prisoners, specially trained to fight. Equipped with different weapons and costumes, they were pitted against each other, and sometimes against animals too.

Gladiators were the superstars of Roman times. If they won enough contests, they could win their freedom. But it was a brutal and bloody sport; gladiators were expected to fight to the death.

This mosaic is from Rudston villa, near Hull. The chariot racer is waving a palm leaf, showing he has won.

High drama

Theatrical shows were another popular form of public entertainment in Roman times. Plays known as tragedies told classical tales of the gods, while comedies were about ordinary people and could be very rude. To compete with the thrill of the games, these dramatic performances included all kinds of special effects, music, dancing and sometimes very realistic violence.

A day at the races

The Britons were skilled in the use of chariots in warfare, so they probably relished the Roman sport of chariot racing for entertainment. Racers hurtled around a large track at breakneck speeds, crashing into one another to try to throw their rivals off course.

The worst collisions, known as shipwrecks, were often fatal. But the violence wasn't always limited to the racetrack. Charioteers raced in teams and serious arguments and even brawls often broke out between fans of opposing sides.

Different strokes

There were several types of gladiators, with different costumes and weapons.

A *murmillo* had a sword, a shield and a helmet with a fish crest.

A *retiarius* fought with a net and a trident.

A *Thracian* had a curved dagger and a small, round shield.

A *Samnite* had a sword, a shield and a helmet with a visor.

41

Gods and goddesses

The official Roman religion was made up of many gods and goddesses. As long as the Britons worshipped the Roman gods, they were free to follow as many other religions as they liked. So, they kept their own local gods alongside Roman ones, as well as adopting exotic cults from all corners of the empire.

The Romans had themselves adopted most of their gods and goddesses from the Greeks, but changed their names to Roman ones.

Each god and goddess was said to control a different aspect of life. The king of the gods was Jupiter. People prayed to Mars for success in war, to Minerva for wisdom, and to Venus for love. Many emperors were even declared gods when they died, and statues and temples to them were built all over the empire. Praying to them was a mark of respect for the Roman rulers.

This is how the temple to the Emperor Claudius in Colchester would have looked before it was destroyed by Boudicca's army in the year 60.

The base of this temple is still standing today, under Colchester Castle. The castle was built on top around a thousand years after the temple was destroyed.

People gather outside the temple for public ceremonies – most of the time, only priests are allowed inside.

Sacred rituals take place at an altar, where offerings are burned to the gods.

Mix 'n' match religions

Like the Romans, the Britons also worshipped many gods and goddesses. Some Roman settlers adopted these local gods, often matching them to Roman gods with similar characteristics. Over time, the identities of these gods became blurred and new ones emerged, combining aspects of native and Roman gods.

Sacred rituals

Religious rituals took place at temples that housed statues of the gods. On a special holy day there was a procession of priests and musicians playing on pipes and tambourines. When they reached the temple, an animal – oxen, goats and chickens were common offerings – was sacrificed on an altar outside. People also gave other, simpler gifts to the gods, including cakes, wine and money.

This is part of a bronze sculpture of Sulis-Minerva found at Bath. Her identity combined Sulis, a local water nymph, and Minerva, the Roman goddess of wisdom.

Exotic cults

Roman soldiers came to Britain from all corners of the empire, bringing their religions with them. These included devotion to mother goddesses, such as Isis from Egypt and Cybele from Turkey. Mithras, the Persian god of light, was particularly popular with soldiers and merchants, because he stood for discipline and fair play. Only men could worship Mithras. They met in underground temples, where they underwent all kinds of initiation rituals, including being locked in a tomb for several hours.

The Druids

The Romans accepted the Britons' religion, but not their priests, the Druids.

In the year 60, the legions stormed Anglesey, the Druids' holy island, and killed almost all of them.

Early Christians

Gradually, many people began to lose faith in the state gods and goddesses. Instead, they turned to new religions brought to Britain by Roman soldiers from the Middle East. The most popular was Christianity. Unlike previous religions, this new faith had strict rules on how its followers should live, and it offered them life after death.

Christianity began about 2,000 years ago when a Jew named Jesus started preaching in Judea, a small Roman province in the Middle East. After he died, his followers continued to teach his ideas. By the end of the 2nd century, Christianity had spread right across the Roman empire.

The Romans banned this new religion and persecuted Christians for refusing to worship the Roman emperor or the state gods. Christians risked flogging, prison and even execution if they were caught. But many continued to meet and worship in secret. Some of them even set aside a room in their home to use as a church.

God's work

In the 5th century, Patrick, a Romano-British Christian, sailed to Ireland to spread Christian teachings. He became St. Patrick, the patron saint of Ireland.

This is a reconstruction of Lullingstone Roman Villa, in Kent. The side has been cut away so you can see the church inside. The walls are decorated with paintings of religious images and symbols.

In the cellar, historians found what they think is a pre-Christian shrine.

These painted figures from the house church at Lullingstone show how early Christians prayed, with their arms outstretched.

Dying for the cause

In the early 3rd century, a soldier named Albanus was beheaded after giving shelter to a Christian priest who was fleeing persecution. He was probably the first Romano-Briton to have died for his faith. Many years later, Albanus was made a saint and his town, *Verulamium*, was renamed St. Albans.

The most brutal persecution took place a century later, when Emperor Diocletian ordered the deaths of thousands of Christians across the Roman empire.

A Christian emperor

In 306, there was a new emperor, named Constantine, who was sympathetic to Christians. He ended the persecution and later became a Christian himself. Gradually Christianity gained more and more followers, then in 391, the emperor Theodosius declared it the official Roman faith. Although some people still believed in the old gods, it became illegal to worship them and many old temples were turned into churches.

This mosaic, from a Roman villa in Dorset, is the oldest picture of Jesus Christ in Britain. Behind him are the first two letters of Christ's name in Greek.

45

New food

The Romans introduced the Britons to many new vegetables, including...

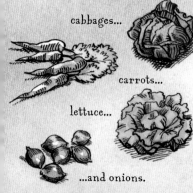

cabbages...

carrots...

lettuce...

...and onions.

Before this, Britons mainly ate bread, stews and porridge.

This scene shows how a Romano-British farm estate would have looked in the 2nd century.

Country life

During the Roman occupation, dozens of new towns and army forts were built around Britain. The thousands of people who lived in them didn't have the time or space to grow their own food. But the new road network made it much easier and quicker for farmers to transport their produce to these new consumers. For the first time, farming became big business.

Farming innovations

To supply the growing demand, agriculture became more intensive. Farmers began to rotate their crops – planting a field with corn one year and beans the next – to keep the soil rich. The Romans developed more efficient tools and brought new ideas about fertilizers, land drainage and animal breeding.

Only an exceptionally wealthy family could afford a palatial *villa*, like the one on this hilltop.

Grand designs

Before Roman times, Britain's farmland was divided into small farms, owned and farmed by individual families and tribes. But, as farming became more commercial, many wealthy landowners bought up huge estates. The peasants no longer owned their own land, but rented homes on the estate they farmed. This social system lasted in England and Wales for the next thousand years.

As farms grew, so did the farmers' houses. Soon after the Roman invasion, many of them began to adopt a more Roman lifestyle, replacing their round houses with rectangular huts in the Roman style, with extra floors, verandahs and annexes. By the late 2nd century, many of these farmhouses had become lavish mansions, which the Romans called *villas*.

The chase

Hunting was central to country life in Roman Britain, both as a sport and for catching food.

This mosaic from Chedworth Roman Villa shows a hunter carrying a deer's antler and a hare. Hunters also chased wild boar and birds.

Pigeons are kept to use as food in winter.

Bees are kept in beehives for their honey.

Oxen do heavy work.

Hens and ducks are kept for their eggs and meat.

Feasting and fun

Whether they lived in a sprawling villa in the countryside or a large town house, known as a *domus*, Roman Britain's rich and famous lived in homes that were luxurious, even by today's standards. For men such as government officials and merchants, it was important that their homes reflected their wealth and status. So they had opulent living rooms, stylish dining rooms and formal courtyard gardens.

On the menu

As well as many types of meat, seafood, grain, fruit and vegetables still widely eaten today, the Romans also ate some dishes that were exotic, to say the least.

1,000 larks' tongues

Stuffed dormice

Sea urchins

Home entertainments

Wealthy Romans loved to show off their beautiful homes by throwing extravagant dinner parties that began early in the evening and could last long into the night. Guests removed their sandals at the door and had their feet washed by a slave, before being shown to their places. They ate reclining on cushioned couches arranged in a horseshoe shape in the dining room.

The meal opened with appetizers such as salads, eggs, oysters and sardines. For the main course, fish, meat and poultry were served, often with strong sauces made from fish or spiced fruit. This was followed by fruit, nuts and honey cakes, all washed down with plenty of wine.

Music and dancing

Hosts often hired performers to entertain their dinner guests with music and dancing. Some rich Romans did learn how to play musical instruments, but they thought it was undignified to play in public. So most professional musicians and dancers were slaves. The instruments they played included pipes, lyres (small harps) and tambourines.

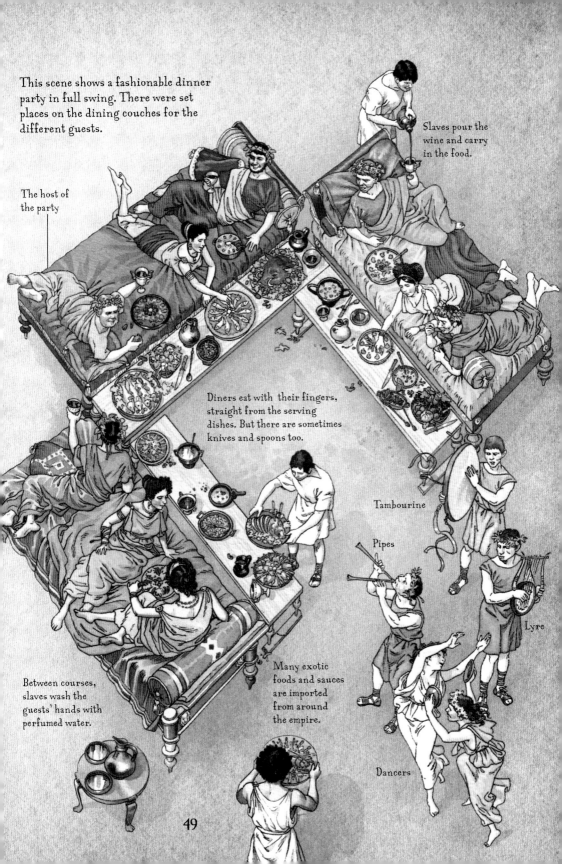

This scene shows a fashionable dinner party in full swing. There were set places on the dining couches for the different guests.

Slaves pour the wine and carry in the food.

The host of the party

Diners eat with their fingers, straight from the serving dishes. But there are sometimes knives and spoons too.

Tambourine

Pipes

Lyre

Between courses, slaves wash the guests' hands with perfumed water.

Many exotic foods and sauces are imported from around the empire.

Dancers

Family affairs

In the days before the Romans came, some British women, like Boudicca, held powerful positions. But under Roman rule a woman's place was far more limited. She was expected to stay at home and look after the family.

A typical Romano-British household was made up of the head of the family – the *paterfamilias* – his wife and children and his sons' wives and children. It was the father's duty to lead the rituals that marked the most important events in family life: births, marriages and deaths.

The fragrant plant myrtle, shown here, was often used to make wedding garlands.

In this Roman wedding scene, the *pronuba* (usually the mistress of the house or the bride's mother) is presiding over the ritual clasping of the couple's hands.

Married life

When a Romano-British girl was about 13, her family arranged a marriage for her. Wedding customs varied, but some British families adopted the Roman way of getting married. On the morning of a typical Roman wedding, the bride dressed in a long white tunic with a saffron-yellow veil over her head. Then the family decked the house in ribbons and garlands of flowers.

Wedding vows

When the groom and the guests arrived, a priest sacrificed an animal to the gods. After signing the marriage contract, the bride and groom joined their right hands to say their vows. The ceremony was followed by a feast and a procession to the groom's house.

50

When a child is born

A wife's main duty was to produce lots of children – preferably boys who might bring prosperity to the family. Childbirth was a risky business in Roman times, and shrouded in mystery. During pregnancy, women prayed to the gods for safe delivery of a healthy baby.

When a baby was born, it was placed at the feet of the *paterfamilias*, who lifted it up as a sign that he welcomed it into the family. At nine days old, the baby was named and given a lucky charm, called a *bulla*, to ward off evil spirits.

Ancient medicine

In Roman times, people knew little about how the body works or what causes diseases. Most doctors worked for the army and could only perform very basic operations. So, if a member of the family fell ill, he or she was usually treated by a friend with a little knowledge of herbal remedies. Many people thought sickness was a punishment from the gods. So they tried to find a cure by chanting spells or praying to particular gods with special healing powers.

Funeral fashions

When a person died, the family chanted a funeral song while the body was washed and clothed.

The body was carried to the cemetery outside the town walls, followed by mourners and musicians.

Sometimes, the body was cremated and the ashes put into a pot, like this one decorated with a face.

All these herbs were used to make medicines in Roman times.

Fennel was supposed to calm the nerves.

Sage was used in cough mixtures.

Rosemary was used in remedies for bad eyesight.

Mustard seeds were used to treat snakebites.

Lemon balm was believed to cure headaches.

Growing up

This scene shows a typical Roman school, known as a *ludus*.

A teacher was called a *pedagogus*. Many were slaves from Greece.

Older students read history and literature from scrolls...

...wrote on wax tablets

...and did sums on a counting frame, or *abacus*.

Younger children scratched letters onto bits of broken pot.

Being a child in Roman times probably wasn't much fun. As soon as they were old enough, most boys were sent to work, while their sisters stayed at home to learn how to spin wool, weave, sew and cook. But, if the family could afford it, at the age of seven, boys and a few girls were sent to a school called a *ludus*.

Before the Romans came, the Britons taught their children by word of mouth, passing on stories, poems and songs about the heroic deeds of their ancestors. Instead of writing these stories down, they learned them all by heart. And because they didn't keep written records of their history and literature, this meant British scholars, such as the Druid priests, were able to keep their learning and ideas secret from outsiders.

Text messages

But after the Romans arrived teaching was based on writing. Paper hadn't been invented yet, so there weren't any books. Instead, children read the works of Roman and Greek authors from large scrolls, made from papyrus reeds. But papyrus was expensive, so they used other surfaces to write out their lessons.

The youngest children tried out their letters by scratching them onto old bits of broken pot. When they were older, they used a pointed tool, called a *stylus*, to scratch words onto a wooden tablet coated with wax. Once the tablet was full, pupils used the flat end of the *stylus* to smooth out the wax, ready to start again. Older children sometimes also wrote on thin sheets of wood, using metal pens dipped in ink.

Great expectations

Most children finished school at age 11. But boys from affluent families went on to advanced studies at a school called a *grammaticus*. There, they were groomed for high-flying careers in law or politics. Their lessons included Greek and Roman literature, history, geography and mathematics. Another important subject was public speaking, or rhetoric, which the Romans considered a crucial skill for any official job.

Marbles and games pieces were made from glass, bone or pottery.

The word

To be successful in Roman times, the Britons didn't just need to learn how to read and write; they also had to learn a new language. Lessons were taught in Latin, the official Roman language of government, law, the army, business and trade. In the towns, younger people picked up Latin and passed it on to their children, but Celtic languages were still common at home and in rural areas.

This is a selection of Roman pens, wooden writing tablets and an ink pot with its owner's name, *Iucundus*, scratched onto it.

Child's play

But childhood in Roman Britain wasn't all work and no play. Many children had simple toys, such as dolls, model animals and marbles, which they often had to make for themselves. They also played games that would be familiar today, including dice, board games, hide-and-seek, ball games and hopscotch.

53

Tiny tiles

Decorative floors known as *mosaics* were often laid in grand homes and public buildings. They were made up of thousands of tiny glass, stone or pottery tiles, or *tesserae*, set in concrete.

Designs ranged from simple geometric patterns and borders, to elaborate scenes from ancient myths.

Complex designs were put together in wooden frames in the craftsmen's workshops. These were set in position, then simpler sections were completed on site.

This floor mosaic, from Bignor Roman Villa in Sussex, shows Venus, the goddess of love. The style is typically Roman.

Arts and crafts

Wealthy Romano-Britons loved to fill their homes with beautiful things. They paid highly skilled craftsmen to produce mosaics, sculptures, and beautiful artifacts that we can still admire today.

Artistic styles in Roman Britain combined two very different traditions. The British style was usually abstract, with intricate curved patterns. The Romans, on the other hand, liked to depict the gods, people and nature. Under Roman influence, British craftsmen began to illustrate the same subjects as the Romans, but often using a more decorative style.

This huge dish has the head of the sea god Neptune in the middle. At over 60cm (23in) across, it's the most spectacular piece from a hoard of Roman silverware found by a farmer at Mildenhall in Suffolk in the 1940s.

The treasure was buried at the end of the 4th century, like many other Romano-British hoards. Perhaps people hid things to keep them safe from raiders.

Sculpture

There were many uses for sculptures in Roman Britain. Government officials employed skilled sculptors to produce grand, larger-than-life statues of Roman emperors and dramatic carved battle scenes to grace town squares and public buildings.

At the market, ordinary people could buy small mass-produced statuettes of gods to place in shrines in their homes. Sculptors also applied their skills to decorating people's gravestones with pictures of the dead person at work or with their families.

Gorgeous glass

By the 1st century, the Romans had learned how to blow and shape molten glass to make anything from a simple jar to an exquisite drinking goblet. Plain glass bottles were manufactured cheaply in bulk. Precious glass objects could be made from tinted, engraved or even gilded glass. They were used at elegant dinner parties or put in people's graves as funeral offerings.

This delicate glass jug was discovered in a Roman grave in Buckinghamshire.

Ruling Britannia

In the 180s, trouble flared up once again in Britain, and once again it came from the north. The tribes of Scotland had been reasonably peaceful for 20 years, but now they crossed Hadrian's Wall to invade Roman territory. The Roman army in Britain crushed the rebellion, and the emperor Commodus was so pleased with the victory that he gave himself the title *Britannicus*, meaning Conqueror of Britain.

Power struggles

But this unrest had come at a time when Roman power was weakened by political turmoil back in Rome. By 192, Commodus had been assassinated, and power struggles continued over the next century, as rivals competed to become emperor. Meanwhile Britain, and its strong Roman army, had become an attractive prize for those aiming for total control of the Roman empire.

Divide and rule

After Commodus' death, legions from the different Roman provinces each proclaimed their own leader as the new emperor of Rome. One of them was the British governor, Clodius Albinus, but he was beaten to the top job by Septimius Severus, a general from Africa.

Severus arrived in Britain in 208 and spent three years sorting out all the problems. To prevent future governors becoming too powerful, he split Britain into two provinces: *Britannia Superior* and *Britannia Inferior*. They had a governor each, based in London and York.

Odd obsessions

Several of the Roman emperors closely connected to Britain had some bizarre hobbies.

Commodus liked to dress up as the legendary hero Hercules.

Septimius Severus wouldn't do anything without consulting his horoscope first.

And Constantine spent a lot of time and effort moving buildings from Rome to Constantinople.

This is a Roman painting showing the emperor Septimius Severus with his wife Julia Domna and his two sons, Caracalla (on the left) and Geta.

You can see that Geta's face has been scraped off. This is because, after Septimius Severus died, Caracalla killed Geta and had all traces of him wiped out. Caracalla then declared himself emperor.

Rebel empire

After Severus died, the empire was plunged into civil war again. The fighting went on for fifty years and became known as the Anarchy. During this turbulent period, Britain, Gaul, Spain and lower Germany broke away to form an independent Gallic empire. It lasted 14 years until 273, when a strong emperor, Aurelian, brought the provinces back under Roman control.

This gold coin shows Aurelian on the front...

Minted

During the Anarchy, steep price rises and high taxes drove some people to forge counterfeit coins. Aurelian made reforms to prevent this. Like many Roman emperors, he also used the coinage to boost his public image. Every coin showed his portrait on one side and publicized his latest achievements on the other. This showed the people who was boss and kept them up-to-date with the news.

...and his victory over the rebel provinces on the back.

New invaders

Near the end of the 3rd century, tribesmen from northern Germany, called Saxons, launched a number of pirate raids on ships in the North Sea. To protect themselves from further raids, the Romano-Britons built a string of forts along the coast from Brancaster in the east all the way to Portchester in the south. They called it the Saxon shore.

Compared to the usual Roman forts, the Saxon shore forts varied a lot in shape, their walls were higher and thicker, and they had more lookout towers.

Emperor of Britain

Carausius, a Roman admiral in charge of the fleet in the English Channel, was responsible for building some of the Saxon shore forts. But in 286 he was accused of keeping some of the Saxon pirates' bounty for himself. To avoid being punished, he seized control of Britain and proclaimed himself Emperor. While the Saxon shore forts kept the Saxons out, they probably helped Carausius to fend off the Romans too, for a while.

The Saxons' name is thought to have come from the weapon they used – a type of knife known as a *seax*.

Portchester Castle, near Portsmouth, is one of the Saxon shore forts built by Carausius in the 280s.

In this photograph, you can also see a castle (in the bottom left corner) and a church that were built inside the Roman walls in the 12th century.

Carausius and his independent British empire held out for ten years – until the Romans invaded and recaptured Britain. This time, the Romans divided the land into four provinces, with new capitals at Cirencester and Lincoln.

Imperial York

In 306, the emperor Constantius, who had been leading the Roman army in Britain, died in York, surrounded by his family. His son Constantine was immediately declared emperor by his troops in York – although he had to return to Rome and fight a rival before he could take control of the empire. Like Commodus before him, Constantine took the title *Britannicus*, showing that he had won a victory in Britain, though history doesn't record the details.

The trouble continues

For the emperors after Constantine Britain became more and more of a problem. They had to face increasing attacks from beyond the frontier, as well as rebellions inside the province. But Britain wasn't the only part of their empire that was causing concern.

By the end of the 4th century, Roman power over western Europe was starting to decline. A succession of weak emperors and attacks on the frontiers had taken their toll. So the Romans began to withdraw troops from Britain in order to defend other parts of their empire. Even the city of Rome itself was under threat. Finally, after four centuries, Roman rule in Britain came to an end.

Eboracum

The city of York – known to the Romans as Eboracum – in the north of England was made the capital of *Britannia Inferior* in the 3rd century.

It was unusual that Constantine was declared emperor there – normally the only city where this could take place was Rome.

But Constantine wasn't the first emperor to spend time in York. The earlier emperor, Septimius Severus, spent three years ruling the empire from York, until he died there in 211.

Decline and fall

Despite the turmoil elsewhere, Britain was still peaceful and prosperous in the first half of the 4th century. Craftsmen were building lavish villas and creating fine mosaics and furnishings to put in them.

By the beginning of the 5th century, the Saxons had intensified their raids in the south of Britain. The north was also under increasing attack too, from Caledonians and Picts from Scotland and tribes from Ireland breaking through Hadrian's Wall. In 410, Rome itself was overrun by Germanic tribes. The emperor, Honorius, told Britain it would have to fend for itself.

Although Roman rule was over, the Roman way of life lingered on in parts of Britain for the next 150 years. But gradually, more and more people started leaving the towns to live in the country, and once-grand public buildings were falling into disrepair. In the north and west, little changed. People continued to live as they had before the Romans, keeping their languages and culture alive.

But, in the 5th and 6th centuries, southern Britain came under new influences. Invading tribes of Saxons, Angles and Jutes, from what is now Germany, settled down and formed their own kingdoms. It was the beginning of a new age for Britain.

This is a modern painting showing a gang of Saxon raiders attacking a walled city in Roman Britain.

Map of Roman Britain, 43-410

This picture map shows the most important Roman landmarks, towns and roads in Britain.

Legionary fortress
Major fort
Saxon shore fort
Villa
Temple
● Capital
● Major town – *colonia* or *civitas* capital (with Roman name)

Inchtuthil

Antonine Wall
Bearsden Bar Hill

Newstead

CALEDONIANS AND PICTS

Carrawburgh Wallsend
Housesteads Chesters
Hadrian's Wall
Birdoswald Corbridge South Shields
Vindolanda Newcastle-upon-Tyne

Hardknott
Ambleside

BRIGANTES

Aldborough
(*Isurium Brigantum*)

Rudston

York
(*Eboracum*)

Brough
(*Petuaria Parisorum*)

Anglesey
Caernarfon
(*Segontium*)

DRUIDS

Chester (*Deva*)

Wroxeter
(*Viroconium Cornoviorum*)

Lincoln
(*Lindum*)

Brancaster

Caistor
(*Venta Icenorum*)

Leicester
(*Ratae Coritanorum*)

BOUDICCA AND THE ICENI

Burgh Castle

Ermine Street

Fosse Way

Watling Street

CARATACUS AND THE CATUVELLAUNI

Carmarthen
(*Moridunum*)

Caerwent
(*Venta Silurum*)

Gloucester (*Glevum*)

Chedworth

Caerleon (*Isca*)

Woodchester
Lydney Cirencester
Uley (*Corinium*)
Bath
(*Aquae Sulis*)

Cardiff

Colchester
(*Camulodunum*)

Walton Castle

St. Albans
(*Verulamium*)

Bradwell-on-Sea

London
(*Londinium*)

Canterbury

Reculver
Richborough

Lullingstone

Dover
(*Dubris*)

Silchester
(*Calleva Atrebatum*)

Winchester
(*Venta Belgarum*)

Low Ham

Bignor

Lympne

Hinton-St-Mary

Pevensey Castle

Exeter
(*Isca Dumnoniorum*)

Dorchester
(*Dumovaria*)

Brading

Fishbourne
Portchester Castle

61

Index

Acknowledgements

Every effort has been made to trace and acknowledge ownership of copyright. If any rights have been omitted, the publishers offer to rectify this in any future editions following notification. The publishers are grateful to the following individuals and organizations for their permission to reproduce material on the following pages: (t=top, b=bottom, l=left, r=right)

Cover (bl) © Stephen Mulcahey/Alamy, **(br)** © Jochen Tack/Alamy, **(tr)** © Robert Preston/ Alamy; **p1** © The Trustees of the British Museum; **p2-3 (background)** © Nigel Hicks/Alamy, **(b)** © Charles and Josette Lenars/Corbis; **p8 (tl)** © British Museum/HIP/Topfoto; **p8-9 (b)** © Butser Ancient Farm, www.butser.org.uk; **p14-15** © Charles and Josette Lenars/ Corbis; **p16 (tl)** © British Museum/HIP/Topfoto; **p16-17** © Skyscan/Corbis; **p17 (br)** © Philippa Walton, Courtesy The Portable Antiquities Scheme, with thanks to Bob Middlemass and Rolf Mitchenson; **p19 (br)** © The Trustees of the British Museum; **p20-21** © National Museum of Wales; **p22-23 (b)** © Ian West/Alamy; **p23 (tr)** © Museum of London/HIP/Topfoto; **p25** Ronald Sheridan@Ancient Art & Architecture Collection Ltd; **p26-27 (b)** © Museum of London; **p28 (t)** © Ellice Milton/2006 Topfoto, **(bl)** © Gwynedd County Council; **p30-31 (b)** © Adam Woolfitt/Corbis; **p31 (tr)** © The Trustees of The British Museum; **p32** © English Heritage Photo Library/ Illustrator Judith Dobie/Bridgeman Images; **p33 (br)** © C.M.Dixon/Ancient Art & Architecture Collection Ltd; **p36 (l)** © Museum of London; **p37 (t)** The Manchester Museum, The University of Manchester; **p38 (tl)** © British Museum /HIP/Topfoto, **(bl)** © The Trustees of The British Museum, **(tm)** © Museum of London/Bridgeman; **p39 (r)** ©Museum of London/HIP/Topfoto; **p41 (tr)** © Hull and East Riding Museum, Humberside/Bridgeman; **p43 (tr)** © R. Sheridan/Ancient Art and Architecture Collection; **p44** © Peter Dunn/English Heritage; **p45 (t)** © The Trustees of The British Museum, **(br)** © Crown copyright. NMR; **p47 (tr)** © Topfoto; **p51 (r)** © National Museum of Wales; **p53 (br)** © The British Museum/ HIP/Topfoto; **p54** © Ancient Art and Architecture Collection; **p55 (t)** © The British Museum/ HIP/Topfoto, **(br)** © The Trustees of The British Museum; **p57 (t)** © Staatliche Museen, Berlin/ Bridgeman, **(br)** © The Trustees of The British Museum; **p58 (b)** © Skyscan/Corbis; **p60 (b)** © Museum of London/HIP/Topfoto.

Digital design by John Russell. Picture research by Ruth King.